Contents

About Moi

Hey there. Welcome to the complicated brain of Adrian. My buddies call me A.D. so feel free. Who am I? Well.... I'm nobody really. Just a dude who observes the world on a daily basis and need somewhere to dump his thoughts like Marvel's The Watcher. I observe and I record. These pages will be where I will dump gallons of thought but there will be no pollution. No birds covered in oil. Just different point of views and opinions (opinions have been known to smog up the air we breathe but I will try to keep it as filtered as possible, so you don't have to wear white masks).

This is the 2nd volume of my Observation series. Here, I will be writing about my observations of people and how we interact and are molded. I will be documenting how I view racial issues and how I think people view each other. This will not be for the sensitive but will be for those who are looking for a different perspective. I hope you enjoy. Please enjoy. I have 20 mouths to feed. Also, look out for my first volume on Relationships and be on the watch for futher observations on Religion, Politics and Mental Health. You may now proceed to blow your mind but not too early or else you won't be able to finish the book. Duh.

People

Ah yes. People. The world's version of Marmite or pineapple on pizza. You either love them or hate them. Hell, some people even hate full groups of people while others love everybody and everything and that's ok (it's not ok to hate whole races. Stop it. Just… stop it). People are a complicated and intricate bunch. Humans have the ability to show great intelligence, compassion, and empathy and at the same time, humans have the capacity to display rank hatred and ignorance. How can this be? Howwww? Not only that, humans are generally divided on social, racial or class lines (sometimes all the above) along with border lines and all sorts of other lines. There are also circles. We also have the ability to come together, get over our "differences" and coexist as best friends, family friends, couples. It's a beautiful thing. Well to me. Some people recoil in horror at the mere thought of it. They froth and shake their fists at the sky. Why is there such a huge contrast in attitudes among each other (and everything in between)? How can there be such division among the same species, whose only differences are melanin or lack thereof, language and culture? And how is it that different races and peoples can coexist just fine (mainly on an individual level)? Well, I've been wearing my observing specs again and here is what I've witnessed. Prepare yourselves…. for many paragraphs. This might take a while.

This Box is Too Small

First off, let me start by saying, I am black. That is the box I was assigned when I was born. It is also the color of my skin (some would say it's brown, but I will get to this later…or not). My skin is such because of genetics. I happen to produce more melanin, hence my hair, eyes, and tone. Now, this is not to say because I am black that my features are set in stone. Traverse the world and you will see peoples with my shade or even darker with blonde, curly hair or blue/green/hazel eyes. I had zero choice as to what color I would be and that's ok. Nothing wrong with more melanin. Comes in handy when I'm basking in the sun. I'm leading to something. Don't worry. Be patient.

Regardless of genetic diversity, when you hear black or white, you think one specific thing or preset behaviors. These are the boxes that we reside in from the absolute moment we are brought into this world. The black box (no we don't record anything before a disaster) and the white box. There is also the Asian box, Middle Eastern box, and Latin box. This all leads to my very first point of this chapter. Do you know what else I or we had no control over at a young, wee age? Our minds. Our thinking. Our thoughts. No child is born with black/white/Asian thoughts. We are just born in the shell of the race that birthed us. We are then molded and influenced by our parents and the environment around us. Now, this is where the social boxes come in. The

first stage of the box creation is manipulation and inception. People are not a color. They have to be made to BELIEVE that they themselves are a color and accept that belief, just like in the movie Inception (I have probably watched that movie 1000 times. It is the best movie ever and I will battle anyone who disagrees). Once this is achieved, it makes it easier to plant the thought in other people, the observers. How is this done you ask? You ask a lot of questions. I don't like this pressure. But I like you so, I'll answer. Influence and environment. Let's start with a race. My own. Yaaay.

Hey there. Yes you, the one reading this book. What do you think when you hear "black person"? What characteristics, behaviors and attitudes come to mind when you hear "black"? It's not a trick question and no I don't have someone spying on you, ready to pounce if you say something un-pc. It's safe. I promise. Most people have a default set of thoughts when they hear black, white, Asian and even with religions such as Muslim or Christian. Those preset thoughts are stage 2 of inception. They have to be fed to you from somewhere though.

Let's delve into this, shall we? I will be the guinea pig. I was born in good ole London, Blighty. I lived in a family house, far away from stereotypical influences. I was a boisterous young lad at school, being 3 years old and all. I was also the only black kid at my school. Shouldn't have been an issue.

I was only 3 for gosh sakes. But I was an energetic (and by energetic, I mean absolute terror) 3-year-old. I remember being given time out, being told off, chased, punished. Man, it was pure entertainment. When I reached five, I was taken to Barbados (where I currently reside). I always wondered why this was. As I got older, I became more curious as to why that was the case so, I asked my aunt about it. Turns out, my minders and teachers were convinced that this naughty 3-year-old would grow up to be a criminal warlord and they even made sure to say it over and over to my parents and to me.

My family was not too thrilled with the possibility of me being molded by negative reinforcements, so I was shipped off to Barbados by FedEx. I'm kidding. It was UPS. Why am I telling you this? I want to illustrate how, at a young age, children can be molded by adults, based on how they view them or from their own personal beliefs and biases about a particular person or people. Moving on.

So here I am in sunny Barbados with a thick Londoner accent. My influences are different now. The accents are different. The way of life is different, and it is a predominantly black island. Life proceeded, but my accent didn't. Within 2 weeks of living in Barbados, I picked up the rawest Barbadian accent ever witnessed by man. The influence was great. I was known as the Englishman at school

because of where I was born, but I was never placed in a stereotypical box. I was always considered Barbadian and Adrian. I was never aware of any boxes period. I just lived, enjoyed life, enjoyed the music and Barbadian culture of the Island and kept living. This all has a point. Hold your horses.

As time went on, so did advancements. Our little island was soon going to be influenced by cable TV. At first, it started out with 5 channels. Ah, the nostalgia. Watching TNT, Cartoon Network, Lifetime (this one was usually skipped except when Supermarket Sweep was on), ESPN and our own Channel 8 (which was and is as entertaining as waiting times at the bus station. They're long).

Watching Cartoon Network and ESPN really molded me to be the person I am today or at least partly. I was always a comedian who liked to make people laugh. Programs such as What a Cartoon sharpened my skills and sucked air from my own lungs as I laughed in such a manner that would have made The Joker shed a tear. I began to cultivate a love for Basketball and Baseball from watching ESPN. These 2 sports soon began to overtake my love for our national sport, cricket (oh, and because the West Indies cricket team started to go south like migrating birds). As time continued on its merry way, more and more channels were added. Next in line was MTV. This was my introduction to Hip Hop and alternative music. For years the influential music was Soca, Calypso, and Dancehall (Dub to us Barbadians). Now it was Nas, Jay-Z and The Verve (Bittersweet Symphony will never get old).

Lemming Season

My time in Barbados was drawing to a close. I was about to finish school a model student, far from the criminal I was supposed to be in England, though, it could've easily turned out that way as I lived in areas with questionable influences but was saved by my grandparents as we all moved into a lovely home in a nice area with completely different and positive set of influences, apart from my first encounter with racial issues.

Speaking of, it is ridiculous for a race of people, say Indian, to move to a predominantly black Island and be threatened by their daughter talking to a black kid. Or even associating with anyone black. It's pretty ridiculous and primitive of us as human beings and also feeds into what I will be discussing later, but I digress yet again. Back on track.

Now, where was I? Oh yes. I turned out fine. Yaay. It's around 1998/1999. More and more channels are being introduced. We are now being exposed to sex and violence as easily as we're exposed to air. One channel that really stood out and is a major example in this long ass explanation, was BET. Oh, BET. You had your moments. Your comedy show was hilarious.

More importantly to this subject matter, this was the first channel introduced to Barbados that I would consider one of the recruitment tools for the boxes of influence. The narrative. The Inception. This channel swept into this little Island and said, "Hey! This is what being black is. See this music? Do you see this style and clothing? This attitude? This is what being black is guys. This is what you are supposed to be. Bling Bling y'all. After all, we are called Black Entertainment Television".

At the time, it wasn't really a big deal to me. Everything was the same, everyone was the same and we had a lot more entertainment to keep us from that rubbish sun and outdoors nonsense. Yuk. Who needs air and nature when you can watch it in Standard Definition. Fast forward a bit in time and it was time for me to return the England (not long after the introduction of cable). I'm finally back. Oh boy, I am back in England. Now before I continue, I will share my experience of returning to Barbados for holiday and my observations of Barbados, before I continue on to good ole Blighty.

I'm finally on a plane back to the Island I love after a rough couple of years in England (oh we will get to that shortly). I cannot wait to see my friends, experience the culture that I grew up with, see my family and soak up some sun. The plane lands, my grin spreads so wide that the edges of my mouth touched at the back of my head. Some passengers screamed in horror. Some fainted. Some asked me if I was possessed. The point is, I was happy as hell to be home. I stepped out the plane. The sun caressed my face. It was glorious until it started cooking my ass, prompting me to find the nearest shade/air con/ ice bucket challenge. I got through Customs and into Barbados. It's beautiful. I was finally home. The drive home was nostalgic, bringing back memories of a great childhood that would turn into a nightmare when I returned to England.

Everything seemed to be just the way I left it. Well, it seemed to be. There was something a bit off, but I couldn't put my finger on it. I finally reached home. More memories come flooding back. This is where I left my heart and soul, hung up in a wardrobe, awaiting my return. I install my heart, slipped on my soul. I coughed out some dust, made a terrible joke, recalibrated and started dropping my usual one-liners and silly quips. I was back. I looked on the ground and saw massive weights just lying there. I wondered where they came from. I also realized I felt 100 pounds lighter. Weird. Anyway, I'm veering off course again. Why do you guys keep distracting me? Sheesh. Oh, and by the way, this all has a payoff. It's coming. It's not an Autobiography.

The first thing I did was to make arrangements to see my friends. The time approached to visit one of my best, childhood mates. We hadn't seen each other in ages. He was the first

friend I got to know in that nice neighborhood I spoke of earlier. We met. There is nothing but elation. I looked at him. I said, "It's good to see you, dude. Umm, by the way. Why in the blue hell are you wearing all of that bling like a rapper?" It turned out, he was training to be a rapper. The clothing, the jewelry, the attitude were elements I was NOT used to from my friend. Then it hit me. That's what was different about my beloved little island. There was a culture shift. People were wearing bling, dressing like what they saw on…. BET. There was more Hip-Hop and Rap in the atmosphere instead of the Soca, Calypso, and Dub that dominated the airwaves and speakers throughout Barbados. It further dawned on me that the influence of the newly introduced cable TV and especially BET had changed the perception and attitude of the populace. This was my first observation as to how influence can shape people through imagery and messaging.

Till this day, nothing has really changed. Trap (crap) music is big here along with mumble rap and whatever trash is popular these days and it is shaping and molding a new generation of youth to believe that is who they are and how they can be successful. It is also influencing the attitudes of the youth. They are caring a lot less than when I grew up here. See? I told you this long-winded story would circle back to the main point. And you doubted me. For shame.

11

On a side note, speaking of successful, these messages and images can really mold, influence and shape our minds to believe what we perceive to be the right path to success based on our class and race. For example, the white example of success could be a Steve Jobs or a politician (will not be mentioning names here. Pick any). Maybe an Elon Musk. Hell, Leonardo Di Caprio could be an example of success or even Justin Bieber.

My point is, there would be a wide range of options available for someone to look to in society and media as an inspiration for success. Now, if we were to look at the black examples, it wouldn't be a stretch to say Hip-Hop culture would be one of the main driving forces of influence as to what is a path to success for the black individual. That or being an athlete. That is not to say there aren't other examples to follow, but musician and athlete (and just general entertainer) are the dominating forces in society and media that determine what success is for black people and hence, they are defined by these very examples, which really, is dumb as hell but we'll get to that.

On yet ANOTHER side note, I have an issue with very specific things like Hip-Hop culture (jewelry, dance, style, attitude, etc.) being deemed black culture. This, I must stress, is purely my opinion but I can't see something that barely belongs to black people (Hip-Hop is run by corporations and those

are rarely owned by black people), is as fickle as what's in style at the current moment and really was birthed in one country as being black culture (I am speaking of the current iteration and not the time of B-Boys, conscious Hip Hop and the Pan African movement). Maybe American culture, but not black. I can guarantee you it wasn't black culture in the Caribbean or Africa until the messages and imagery were beamed to those places and picked up like a hermit crab shell. Also, this thing called black culture (what is currently considered black culture) is a tool to change the black man into a barcode or marketing billboard. It can be used to make artists and musicians sell shit to people that can't afford it, or help companies sell their shit through them while handing them some money and telling them that they made it.

It's also a way for corporations to sell a product like a drug, make huge money from it while also defining and demonizing the people who are influenced by such music and see it as a way out of purgatory. In short, sell your soul and the image of your "race" for millions and an easy life. Should it be that way? No. No one thing should define a whole race. That is insanity. No one group of people is a monolith. Everyone is their own individual. Yes, there is pack mentality, but you still have to review each person individually. Unfortunately, we do not live in that world and whole races are defined by the artificial boxes that are created in society because we as humans are too lazy to learn about individuals and are sometimes willfully ignorant.

The Journey

Seeing as I am on Hip-Hop right now, have you ever noticed the journey of some artists as they become successful and their influence and environment changes? (this all ties in. I hope you aren't lost by now). Let's start from the birth stage. P.S. I am only speaking of one type of rapper here. There are countless artists out there that do not tap-dance to the mainstream beat, who have positive messages and are fighting for social change like the Kendricks, J. Coles and Jerus of this world plus the very skilled underground rappers who don't get exposure or radio play. I speak not of these artists for I respect them a lot. Instead, I speak of those who peddle negative and damaging B.S. for a check advance and some gold chains. Here goes.

Rapper/Entertainer signs a deal (to be a Minstrel of course). Rapper releases a video showing off his money, cars, and hoes. Rapper becomes popular and shows his wealth off constantly. Look at his money. Look at his rides. Look at his bling. Look at his designer clothes. He is constantly showing the world that he's balling. Is this bravado or a cry for acceptance and exaggeration to show the world that they have something and are worth something? I tend to think it is the latter.

Imagine growing up poor and in a shitty environment. Let's say this rapper is you for now. You are in your societal bubble where you are bombarded with certain imagery. It's either you need to be bad to succeed in terms of selling drugs, being a bad boy, being violent, being a rapper, etc. The images projected to you tell you that if you are these things, you will get that money and get that life that you see every day. Think of the imagery and influence as if it were a sheep dog, guiding sheep to a specific place. Sheep secluded within a specific field. Doesn't matter though as you will get that social acceptance from your peeps. Everyone wants love and acceptance, and in an environment that is lacking such qualities, you'll do whatever you need to get it.

So now you have a hit song. People love your music. The ladies now love you because hey, you've now subscribed to the Laws of Attraction in a Fickle World newsletter. You show off more valuables as a scream for acceptance by the class of people who hired you and basically run your finances (they see you as a performing clown by the way) and also by your peeps, the hood.

Your hit song becomes a hit album. You are blowing up charts everywhere and influencing a new generation of youth in ignorance, degradation, and violence. You are basically doing the job you were hired to do. You are providing a product that you are told is popular by the people that sign your checks but will never be affected by it. You start dining at the finest restaurants. You buy that Ferrari you can barely afford. You must represent. You have to show society you're a somebody after being a nobody for so long (you're still a clown to the people that hired you and the general public who viral dance to your stuff at their parties and social gatherings but would dial the police if they saw you in their neighborhood. You are a king to those you help influence and you are an inspiration that they can escape their bonds from poverty by being just like you). You start hanging with different crowds. You now rep the hood but you don't hang out there very often because, well, you worked to get out and bring your people out.

A few more hit albums later and you are rubbing shoulders with celebrities and the crème de la crème. You're now on talk shows, programs, in magazines. Hell, now you're in movies. Your influences and environments are changing around you and so are you. Your clothes start to change to reflect your new crowd. You still release an album of trash because you're contractually obligated to, but your image starts to differ from your art. You start sitting with Jack Nicholson at basketball games and showing up to events in the finest Armani suits. The content of your music also changes. It's more… social. Less abrasive. Your music starts to scream, "I'm a multimillionaire and I don't need to tap dance anymore and peddle to make

a buck. I've made it. I am in control of my own destiny".

Your whole lifestyle has changed. Now, what was the purpose of that stroll down story lane? Well, have you ever noticed that transition? Ever wondered why that is? Are your answers influence and environment? Then you would be correct. A cookie is coming your way. Our social surroundings, the people around us and even our lot in life can mold us to what we are. Unfortunately, people do not see this transition and only see the first half of my example. The negative. This is what defines us, and not as an individual as it should, but as a people. A race.

No one is exempt from this. Every race has that stereotype attached to them, some stereotypes being more damaging and harmful than others. My example above also shows how people can be tools to further perpetuate these stereotypes and keep the cycle going and some sections of rap play a huge part of that machine just for a check and some rims. We as humans are a fickle bunch and we focus on the negative portrayal of people to define who we meet. Remember that part earlier in the book where I was supposed to go back to talking about my time in England? Hop into the time machine. We're going back.

This Damn Box Again

It was my time in England that really made me pay attention to human behavior and interaction. I was now in the country of my birth, the box from my youth was there ready for me to step in and be defined by it. Adrian though sits In no box. I have a bad back. Hurts the knees. I was firmly caught between two worlds. The first world was the stereotype world where assumptions of race resided. The box if you will. The other world was one where some from my race accepted the inception of the box and stereotypes and lived their way accordingly.

So, in other words, this is how you are supposed to act vs. this is how you act. I isolated myself for the first 3 years of being in London, jaded by both worlds and unwilling to associate with either. It can get tiring always having to fight people's flawed perceptions of who you are when you're the complete opposite or not relating to others because the consensus is that you are supposed to act like them because you share the same color. Also, a lot of the black youth were really up to no good and fully embraced the box that society presented to them. It was really depressing to be caught in those worlds.

A fine example of this quagmire was at work. My first job in London was in retail in the City. Lord have mercy, the City. This is where I experienced both worlds first hand. Pay attention. This is a perfect account of how we view each other as people.

I hit the ground running in my first job. There I was, a little black boy with a THICK Caribbean accent, ripe for confusing people. I worked hard and was trusted by my peers and managers (for some reason, people trusted me more than usual. Must have been this angelic smile). I won awards for my hard work and really gelled with the team, even though deep down inside I was screaming because I was an introvert working in an industry filled with people (customers).

I always feared for many years what people thought of me as there was always the battle to counter negative depictions and assumptions. I felt awkward and anxious every day, but I sucked it up and did what I had to do. People really warmed to me because I seemed so different from what they were used to. There was the assumption of a lack of education, but I rode that wave like a surfer and always put people in their places. I worked on the floor but managed to get a gig in the stockroom (I really was not an open, outgoing person and struggled to interact with customers). This was perfect isolation where I got to feel relaxed and be away from people, gather my thoughts and listen to my music.

At the time Eminem was taking no prisoners and destroying charts everywhere. His name was on everyone's lips, even those you wouldn't take for ones that liked the genre. Anyway, there I am, playing my crass Eminem CD. My manager passes by, stops and looks at me with a bewildered look. She sternly proclaims, "That song is offensive. You cannot listen to that. Who is that"? Now, I won't lie. I was observant to the fact that white people at the time gave Eminem a free pass so when I heard the question, a smirk formed on my face and I uttered, "It's Eminem (smirk emoticon face). Predictably, her look of shock and horror turned to joy as we discussed how great he was and how great the song Stan was. That smirk stayed on my face till the very end of the conversation and I was allowed to continue listening to this highly offensive CD because it was Eminem (funnily enough, Eminem himself was aware of this hypocrisy and mentioned it in many of his songs).

I found this incredibly fascinating as another colleague was not allowed to listen to his, less offensive Hip-Hop. It was from here that I started to pay attention to EVERYTHING.

My time at this place was littered with silly comments and ignorant mumblings. By the way, I know this is really beginning to look like an autobiography but it's not. Just life examples that fit the subject matter. Now as I was saying, I was born in a tiny town named... just kidding. You can pick the book back up. As I was saying, my 2 most favorite, ignorant comments were, I was selfish for talking the way I talked because it was hard to understand. Umm, this is the way I talk. Haven't you seen my movies? (Samuel L. Jackson

accent). The other example was my absolute favorite. I licked my fingers after this one, it was so... filling. Smack Smack.

There was a young white manager who had recently started that decided she would add to my workload without thought as to what she was doing (this seemed to be a theme in retail where young dumb people were thrust into managerial positions). At the time there was an African cleaner whose last name was Adeyeye if I'm not mistaken. The new manager looked me in the face, in my optical stems, and asked, "Is the cleaner your mother?" Taken aback I replied, "Ummm, no. What makes you think that?" Her reply was one for the ages. She proceeded to say, and I quote, "Because you have the same last names." Now that would be fine and dandy if my name wasn't ARMSTRONG. I proceeded to tell her this and explain that my last name is actually Scottish. Her reply to this was awesome. She said, "Well you know all you people have the same sounding names." Another colleague and I locked eyes in hilarious awe.

What exactly did I just hear? That event was filed away to be used in a book at some point in the future. I might title it, Dumb Shit. It'll be awesome. Now you're probably asking, why the hell did you go through all of that? Well, I did it to point out how people have preconceived notions about others and things without getting to know them and how certain

things that are taboo with one race is acceptable to another.

Now, no race is exempt from this. I had preconceived notions of my own. A new white colleague with a shaved head made me assume he was a skinhead Nazi. He turned out to be the coolest person I had ever met and was just like me, racially ambiguous. He wasn't a white guy. He was just Dave. Another female colleague was just Sarah, whereas I assumed she would be distant and aloof with me as a black guy (this was my own paranoia living in England). Instead, we went on lunch and conversed a lot to the confusion of certain people who thought I probably didn't like white people generally because I didn't like them personally (the certain individuals), but I had my reasons for not liking them as individuals. My experiences showed me how easy it was to judge someone you don't know based on experiences you might have had with someone else who was completely different. It showed me that we as humans can be lazy in our thinking but sometimes it is a defense mechanism so as to not get hurt. It's not right, but it is also understandable.

For all the good one person does, it only takes the actions of an idiot to put a question mark on the one who does good, based on the fact that they share the same race or religion. For all the hard work and trust that I earnt at work, all it took was some guys from a bad area (what was my workplace thinking?) to work for the Christmas period and rob the place, which prompted management to say, let's keep an eye on the black ones, instead of dealing with the individuals who committed the crimes. All it took was for a new set of racist managers to erase the memory of previous white managers that were very helpful and friendly. Us humans default to our preconceived notions way too easily and quickly because what is embedded in our minds is, blacks are criminals and whites are racist. We could see 10 people a day who contradict our thought process and see one example of a person who confirms our flawed thinking and that one will be enough. This is confirmation bias 101.

It can take one mistake to brand you something you are not, for example, a great guy I knew once said the word colored to describe a black woman, and was branded a racist, even though if she had really paid attention and had gotten to know him, she would have seen that he didn't have a racist bone in his body and was a great, friendly guy who just misspoke, which is understandable with all the labels and words that are used to describe fellow humans. Someone could see or hear a story about a single black mother and think to themselves, yuuup, black dads are never around (a standard stereotype). That very same person would have probably passed 15 black fathers that day and it would have never registered. In short, what we believe or whatever or biases

are, they can make us completely blind to reality as we look for the minor percentage to justify and confirm what we think.

I see, Therefore I believe

So, how in the blue hell did it get like this, humans painting each other with a large, stupid brush, us pinning ridiculous stereotypes on one another (I do like fish and steak too ya know. I don't like watermelon and not all white people like mayonnaise and Kale. Oh, and everyone likes chicken because it's tasty. Don't be silly now) and generally seeing each other (race and religion) like a swarm of engineered and well programmed droids that would make SkyNet shed a single, slow-motion tear? Well, the answer is rather complex. You can find it in my other book, coming to a store near you. I'm kidding. Just send $10 through PayPal for the answer. Ok ok. I'm going to get to it. Sheesh. No sense of humor.

I know you are waiting for the answer and here it is. A mixture of isolation, lack of exposure and (drumroll) our favorite word of the book…. INFLUENCE. There is no I in team. We humans love teams be it sports, politics (ohhhh I have a lot to say about this. Don't you worry), or a special club or gathering, we as a species love to congregate to our own. All you have to do is look at any rivalry to see the depths of how tribal we are. In sports, you have massive rivalries like Arsenal FC vs. Tottenham Hotspur and Manchester

United vs. Liverpool (football), The New York Yankees vs. The Boston Red Sox (baseball) and Golden State Warriors vs. Cleveland Cavaliers. Have you ever seen the level of respect and goodwill rival fans show towards each other? Manchester United fans calling Liverpool fans filthy scousers. Liverpool fans calling Manchester United fans dirty Mancs. So much goodwill. So, so much. Actually, they all hate each other and would fight if paths were crossed in a pub.

Have you ever come across a fan of one sport who also likes the rival team as well? What's that you say? Impossible? Crazy? Treacherous? What person in his right mind would support Arsenal and like Tottenham Hotspur (sorry. Let me replace like with, not hate with a burning passion). A Yankee fan who likes The Red Sox? Uggggh. My head hurts. It's unthinkable. I follow football (Of course I do, I'm British) or, as is named in the USA, Socc.... Socce.... give me a minute................... Soccer. Uggggghh. That was painful to say. Witnessing a rival match is a thing of beauty. The Police are there in droves, everyone is separated and ushered into their designated areas and everyone is on edge. The real magic happens in the stadium. Rival fans sing songs at each other that would make their mums either proud or livid that they raised a child with such a filthy mouth that was capable of spouting sharp, crass barbs at another fellow human being. If you're lucky, a fight might break out post-match. Now that's true unity. A group of fans putting aside their differences as people and coming together as supporters to kick the asses of supporters from another team. True unity. Now I'm going to share something with you that might get me killed, or at least have me running for my life. I might have to change my name to Hans Goodfellow and move to Sicily by revealing this but, here goes.

I'm an Arsenal fan and, I don't have an issue with Tottenham (runs for cover. Peeks over the table). Sports is one avenue that truly taps into human tribalism. What I spoke about above is an idea of how incredibly irrational we can get when we become tribal. Think about this for a second. Fans of one team can literally create an image from rumors and conjecture of another team and just like that, anyone who is a supporter of said rival team is automatically that image. It really is ridiculous. Anyway, those filthy Mancs really need to shower. Yuck.

Do you think sports is bad? There might be some unsavory banter, fights, and rowdiness but for the most part, people come together, act a fool, watch a football match, act more of a fool, get drunk, be racist and then go home either elated that their team beat the enemy or are crushed because they lost and the referee missed a stonewall penalty call that would have made it 7-1, giving them the chance to come back from the absolute battering they were receiving. It may

not be ideal, but sports is all fun and games. What about politics though? Or even religion? How about race? Well, I won't be talking about politics and religion in this volume (I have to pad this book out somehow) but I will continue on the theme of race. Oh, I know how some people love talking about race. It makes them feel all fuzzy and warm inside and not defensive at all. At.... all. Right then. Let's get at it.Before I continue down this rabbit hole, I must present this disclaimer.

WARNING. WARNING. THE FOLLOWING IS SATIRE AND WILL POSSIBLY TRIGGER SOME. THE WORDS THAT FOLLOW ARE BASED ON HOW I OBSERVE HOW THE PEOPLE OF THE WORLD VIEW EACH OTHER. REFRAIN FROM SHAKING YOUR FIST OR FROTHING WITH PURE, UNADULTERATED FURY. YOU MAY NOW PROCEED CAUTIOUSLY.

My Team is Better. NO, MY TEAM IS BETTER

Do you remember earlier in the book when I spoke about boxes? You don't? Are you even paying attention? You are, but it was a dead sea scroll length away? Ok, I'll let you off. We as humans have managed to create sports teams of ourselves. We've given each team distinctive characteristics, behaviors, strengths and weaknesses (which is subjective as it's one group assigning these attributes to another group). First up we have the African American/African/Thug

Blacks. This team is known for its offense, be it violence or crime. They are masters at stealing and being up to no good. They are all brawn and no brains, which makes them perfectly suited to sports and heavy lifting. Their defense is their weak spot as it's primarily used to blame social and economic issues for their problems. Their strengths are they are fantastic entertainers who can sing, dance and rap really well. They love materialism (especially jewelry and cars) and money and always strive to get this while also being very lazy. They are also sexed crazed and have large penises. Oh, and they are lousy parents and abandon their children like a pet that got too big and is no longer cute.

Next up are the American/British/Insert any Caucasian country here/Racist/Redneck Whites. This team is known for its excellent defense of justifying atrocities by their own and also justifying racism, classism and all isms possible. They hate anyone that isn't white, which makes them determined and focused on the field. They either live in trailer parks where they have relations with their family or in an office where they are stealing the poor's money. They also believe themselves superior to everything and everyone and deny any ugly history that involves their ancestors. Their strengths are they are super smart, even when they're not and are incapable of doing wrong. Their weaknesses are they are incapable of not stealing from other cultures and appropriating.

Our 3rd team in the Stereotype League is the Arab/Terrorist/ Extremist Muslims. These, like the Whites, are known to hate anyone who isn't like them. They are entirely focused on their goal and wish death on everyone and everything. They hate infidels and are determined to convert everyone and everything to their cause. They look to flood other countries and introduce Sharia Law, which they will use to subjugate and enslave people. They all wear turbans and have beards, are 100% Arab/brown and can be seen from a mile away. All they do is blow stuff up and are a constant threat to civilization and the universe. The Muslims are the Whites main opponent on the field and have had many battles.

The most popular team though are the Freeloading/ Mexican/Shithole Country/Criminal/Illegal Immigrants. They are rapists. They are criminals. I assume some are good people. Their strengths are evasion, stealth, and stamina. They are resourceful and work their asses off but are lazy at the same time. They are all members of gangs, dabble in the drug trade and travel from border to border to drain a country's resources and terrorize its people. Also, no matter how they reached a country, they are most definitely illegal. Ignore those papers and authentic documents.

The Immigrants have been difficult to defeat with rival teams changing their tactics on a regular to try and win a game against them. Oh, and they can't be trusted so whatever tactic they appear to be using, it's the opposite of that. Sneaky buggers.

I could go on and on. There are so many different teams like the Kung Fu/Smart/Chinese to name a few. We all play on this field called earth. Of course, if you believe any of the descriptions used above to describe a people or race then you need to be lobotomized and throw this book out a window now. I'm kidding. Don't be so sensitive. Keep reading, all of you who paid for this book. I don't mean you guys. I love you all. We are basically teams on a field. Of course, each team will see themselves in a completely different light to their rivals. Something tells me they might actually disagree with 99% of their rivals' opinions on them. I wonder why. Hmmm.

I can imagine that each team will describe themselves in the best possible light and rebuke the nonsense that the rival teams say about them. Are the rivals right with their assessment? No. No, they're not. They're idiots. Actually, let's be fair. They are a little bit correct. Don't hurt me. Let me explain. If you look for the worst examples possible in society, you will find your truth. Let's start with each team, shall we? First up:

The Racial Draft
Team Thug Blacks

It would be inaccurate for me to say you would have to look hard to find people of this ilk (according to the colorful description above). Why is this? Well, this team has the most exposure. They are on TV, the news, in entertainment and also on the radio. Most of the time you will see them in their criminal acts, flashing their riches or rapping about some BS that would kill brain cells and make holier than thou people proclaim them to be the devil like The Water Boy's mum. You will see mugshots on the news or in newspapers or hear statistics about how the prison population is disproportionately high with their players. You might even get a story or 2 about a particular city that is rampant with crime or mention of Africa (their training grounds) being a dangerous place.

These players also always complain about being held down by the league. They complain about the referees and bemoan the lack of fair chance. Even worse, they complain about the time their team was banned from the league and made to do menial field work (pitches aren't going to water themselves) for nothing. Well, they say nothing, but we know the truth (?). Instead of complaining, they should pull themselves up by the bootstraps dammit. Get over the psychology of the past. It was 200 years ago. Yes, there were further restrictions on

your past teams and some of your fathers and grandfathers are alive to talk about it, but they should get over it too. Gosh. With so much evidence, how can it be disputed that The Thug Blacks aren't what people think they are? What are you, some apologetic libtard? Hold your horses. Pump your breaks. But your car in park. Put your horse in park. Let us analyze this.

I like to call exposure the "Spotlight" tactic. What is the (Dr. Evil hand quote gesture) Spotlight tactic? It is the act of placing a spotlight on one concentrated place/s or people. "What are you talking about you blithering idiot?", I hear you ask. Let me explain in the best way I know how using an illustration and not of the artistic kind. Sorry to disappoint. Imagine I hated a neighborhood. Just imagine. It sucks. It has 60 houses and I hate them all.

I go into that neighborhood with my trusty camera, looking to document any trouble I find to prove how wretched this neighborhood is. There are 8 houses that are known for questionable practices. They have parties and they are loud. The inhabitants are known for their criminal ways and they constantly play Dubstep. It's a nightmare. The other 52 houses (wait, is it 52? Carry the one. Add 2. Divide by 15. I suck at Math) are relatively quiet, but I don't care. They must be up to no good as well. I just haven't caught them in the act. I hate them all. ARRRGGGHH. I document the 8 houses

of doom. I get every bad act, every crime and indiscretion I can record. Most importantly, I record all the Dubstep they play for that is the gravest crime of all. I take my footage and upload it to YouTube and anywhere I can think of. I market it to get as many views as I can. I have to spread the word. This neighborhood is a dump, and everyone needs to know about it. My videos pick up momentum. Everyone can now see what I see. Word spreads that the town of Townsville is a cesspool and there is evidence to back it up. It's not just 1 house, or 2. It's 8 whole houses. Do you hear me? **EIGHT. EIGHT. EIGHT. EIGHT. EIGHT. EIGHT.EIGHT. EIGHTTTTTTTTT. You are not hearing me. EIGHT. FEAR THIS NEIGHBORHOOD. FEAR IT. EIGGGHTTTTTTT. FEAR THIS NEIGHBOURHOOD. IT'S COMING FOR YOUR CHILDREN AND SOON, IT WILL BE COMING FOR YOU TOO.** The other 52 houses? Oh, just wait. They'll slip up. I'll catch them littering and replay it 50 times. Before you know it, Townsville will be the scourge of the city. No one will trust a Townsvillian again. The eye of distrust and suspicion will follow them wherever they go. My work here is done. 8 has now become 52, and 52 has become 8.

This has been a common tactic used against minorities in any major country and it has been very successful. The Thug Blacks have been tainted with this tactic along with convenient statistics. What statistics do you ask? Well, a common aspect of the Spotlight Tactic is the using of

statistics to make things seem bigger than they are. For example, a common statistic used is the prison population statistic. Almost half of the prison population is black even though they account for a small percentage of the population. Gasp. That is insanity kind sir. These Thug Blacks are a menace to decent society. Their numbers amount to 2 million incarcerated. These animals need to be caged. Well, hold on there Adolf. Let's dig. First things first, 2 million is a large number when you consider the population. P.S., these are USA stats for anyone confused. The thing about percentages is they hide actual numbers very well. If I told you 87% of the crime committed came from Townsville, that would sound insane. But what if I told you, 87% of that crime only came from 8 of 52 houses? Puts things into perspective, doesn't it?

Now, what if I told you some of the recorded crime was for littering? What if I told you littering wasn't an arrestable crime? Notice how the context changes. Now, as I said earlier, 2 million people is a lot of people. That's a lot of team players in one place. But what if I was to tell you the team was made up of 45 million players? That's.... GASP....... 4.4% of the population. Wait. That can't be right. The percentage of black prisoners is a whopping 37%. **THIRTY SEVENNNNNNNNNN.** Don't listen to the 4.4%. That is crazy talk. Look at the bigger number. The Spotlight number. Now, apart from the percentages, what else could

make up that prison population? Well, being targeted could be one thing. If you are out with your camera actively looking for trouble in Townsville then littering will be a crime. Smoking Marijuana would be akin to killing a small puppy named Scrappy (how ironic is it that weed is now sold in stores as if police haven't been locking up black people for owning small amounts?). Resisting arrest while being innocent and not resisting would get you a record. Who told you to be innocent and not resist? No wonder 2 million of you animals are behind bars. There are so many factors involved in the percentages and numbers which lead to inflation of figures. If you want to demonize a group, this is the most effective way of doing it. The poor thug Blacks just can't win a game without being accused of cheating. Too bad they all hail from Townsville as well. That sucks.

Now, this is not to say there aren't gangs and crime happening by some in the black population. It would be naïve to say otherwise. In some parts, it's outright ridiculous the amount of crime there is. Take Chicago. Gang violence has taken a hold on some parts of Chicago and that is always the bigot's go to card for black on black crime. But waaaaaiiiitttt. Noticed I said PARTS of Chicago. Some would have you believe that the whole of Chicago was a war zone. Others would also have you believe that 45 million black people live there. Hmmmm. I wonder why.

In all cities in all of the world, there will be pockets of poor, impoverished neighborhoods where people struggle to make a living, lack opportunities and are infested with crime. But no matter how much people try to bend reality like Neo on Speed (see what I did there?) reality remains straight like a rod. Those examples, just like Chicago, will only ever represent a small percentage of the demographic population. The amount of BS this small percentage does is another thing altogether. This percentage is what Nazi admirers love to massage and serenade, like a full-figured woman that they want to seduce and take to bed, so as to convince others that the people they hate are the worst thing since Coke Zero.

With all of that said, maybe the Thug Blacks do need to cheat to win. Maybe some special system where the Thug Blacks have a level playing ground where they get an opportunity to play their games without judgment, assumption or anything going against their name. Maybe a way to gain points for participation and a medal just for showing up, regardless of who plays better or wins. Heck, the Blacks could possibly win a championship without winning many games. The system could be called…. Favorable Accomplishment. Doesn't quite roll off the tongue, does it? Maybe Affirmative Ac…. nahhhhh. That's even worse. Of course, such a system would automatically negate any real accomplishment that Team Blacks could achieve, being reduced to achievement by Favorable Accomplishment and nothing else. Such a system would cloud Team Blacks with an air of inferiority and would brand other teams superior by definition. I see you wondering what the hell am I talking about. I can see the confusion on your face. Or maybe that's just gas. If it is, remember, silent but deadly. Basically, that system, like Affirmative Action (it is the same damn thing) would be terrible because it would paint Team Blacks as an inherently inferior team that requires a crutch and help just to compete. All of their achievements would then be belittled and passed off as through help and action even if they played their hearts out and won to earn their points. In short, Team Blacks just wouldn't be able to win. Damned if they do, damned if they don't.

Now of course, there is no team, no matter what certain news stations say or what's deemed reality, there are no racial teams. There are individuals of all different thought processes, heart, skills, and actions. Maybe if each person was viewed and judged on their own merit and were allowed opportunity based on said merit without bias, the world would be a better place. What am I saying? Bah. Damn Thug Blacks (shakes fist at black scientist/pilot/policeman). You got that job through Affirmative Action!!

Team Racist Whites

Well, this is going to be awkward. I can guarantee you that this will be the most controversial part of this chapter. Presenting, the most successful and popular team (even though some would have you feel that they're the most hated and discriminated team in the league), the Racist Whites. This team has dominated the league for centuries, taking out one team after another. Even though they are a clear 20 points at the top of the table, they would have you believe they were at the bottom of the league and being held there. This team consists of the players, the coach, the referees, the owners of the team AND league and also some of the marketing and TV rights. They can, on one hand, pick apart a team (sometimes with some dubious calls by the referees) while showing the world a battle against all the odds. This team has the power to hold back other teams, brand them cheats and spoilsports while having the luxury of marketing themselves as the victim. You better not cheat or make a mistake.

Your players better be squeaky clean or else the marketing department of Team Whites will have your ass on record, waiting to play anything negative on the big screen. You've been spotlighted suckas. That's what you get for being flawed. Team Racist Whites, on the other hand, have the perfect weapon in their playbook. This play is called, the benefit of the doubt. If a player from the team is caught cheating, it was

a mistake. Or maybe we all make mistakes and these "small" flaws should be forgiven (flaws that would look like a fire breathing LGBT Godzilla if done on another, "less desirable" team). If a player commits a gross injustice, like say, beat the shit out of someone, there would be punishment., a press conference, some time for it to cool down and blow over, followed by the pardoning and chance to return with open arms and a couple of boos. You better not protest any injustice or wrongdoing if you're on Team Blacks though. What are you, some kind of puppy eating Devil? Go purify yourself in the waters of Lake Minnetonka and don't dare think of having a career again you MONSTER. How dare you protest the rules of the game even though in reality you were not protesting the rules of the game but the injustices that happen within the game. Shaaaaame. SHAAAAMEEEEE.

That's the opposing view of team White Racist, but, what is the reality? Well, (pulls collar) this is going to be awkward. That is not far from reality. That is pretty much how the system is regardless of what anyone thinks. That is the power structure. Where the difference lies is in the crowds. The common folk. The people watching the games. They just want to enjoy a good sports bout. Most don't really care about politics or what's happening on the field/pitch/court. Some are diehard fans of the team and will believe anything that comes from the team and their marketing department.

Hell, they would even help with free marketing and spread that word. Then there are the fans that don't hate Team Thug Blacks or any other team for that matter. They see the discrepancies on the field, the injustices and lopsided nature of the league. It leaves a bad taste in their mouth and an uneasy feeling in their chest. They would love to speak up but, they're surrounded by rabid fans who would turn on them faster than.... than......they will just turn on them, ok? I can't be witty all the time. I'm not a machine you know.

They cheer on while silently feeling guilty for what they see unfold in front of their eyes. Then there are the fans who are vocal and defend the other teams while condemning the nature of how the league is set up and all of the BS they witness on a daily. These will be branded Thug Black (or any team that isn't The Racist Whites) lovers. Traitors. If they become prominent, they would be smeared.

That is the nature of the league. The fans benefit from the support of the team as long as they cheer. The ones who criticize? Well, you can kiss that season ticket goodbye son. I hope you have the sports package at home. By virtue of being white, some players have to deal with being branded racist, even if they do not have a racist bone in their bodies. They have to walk on eggshells and watch everything that comes out of their mouths in fear of offending someone and

being labeled. Other players are racist to their core but play and act all virtuous, frothing at the mouth at being branded what they are (more on this later). As mentioned above, there is no one, set answer. There is only nuance, a forgotten word.

Team Terrorist Muslims

Sigh. These are becoming increasingly harder to write as I go on. Next up is Team Terrorist Muslims. This team is known for its explosive offense and defense and by explosive, I mean they blow shit up. The league has been on alert from its inception because this team just can't play without taking out a few people. They are heretical and view other teams as lesser and heathens. They see themselves as the chosen team and pray to the sports gods for the destruction of the other teams unless their players join their team. They are the villain of the league and revel in their mustache twirling (or beard in this instance) infamy. They're better than you and will remove you from the pitch for a retirement gift of 12 Cheerleaders and a Championship Trophy. Their play style is out of date and out of touch and has no place IN SPORTS DAMMIT.

Now that I've gotten that drivel out of the way, what is the truth about Team Terrorist Muslims? Will I be able to show my face after writing this? Let's test and see. Muslims make up around 2 billion of the earth's...ahem.... I mean the league's total population (players). They reside in

many countries, some majority Islamic while in others they are a minority. They live like any other religious people. They have a belief system and they worship, just like any other religion (I will go in depth when I write my Religion volume. I will for sure not be able to show my face then).

So, why the rank hatred? Well, this team for one possesses a very special resource/s that many of the other teams crave/lust for/would sell their mothers to have. What is this resource? Maybe it's a special "oil" for the joints which allow players to "move" with gazelle-like grace. We'll neeeever know. This resource has driven coaches and executives bat shit crazy. Coaches and managers have been strategically uprooted from Team Muslims, replaced with bootlickers who would give Team Whites whatever they want to make their team better.

Here's the twist. These "allies" also feed their players toxic propaganda and hatred for other teams, which in turn pushes an airheaded idiot to make an illegal play on the field, which in turn gets the team (of mostly clean and fair players) to get banned, fined and vilified. What is the payment? That sweet, sweet oil…ahem…. I mean resource. Keep them vilified and there will always be a reason to "clamp" down on "tyranny" and take what they have. Damn that joint oil. So much turmoil, just for loose limbs.

Apart from having a huge erection for Team Muslim's Joint oil, other reasons for the hatred are the most common and basic, stupid human nature reasons because we have brains with 90% space for rent. Team Terrorist Muslims use a different playbook than the rest of the league, so they are seen as the other and suffer all of the nice add-ons and goodies that come with being the other. They're also brown. I mean, they wear brown uniforms, and there is nothing worse than brown uniforms except, maybe black. Sorry Team Terrorist Muslims and Team Thug Blacks. You should have been born with white uniforms, but you didn't think. You didn't think. Basically, in less than 230 characters, Team Terrorist Muslims have what the league wants, have a different playbook and wear the wrong uniforms and because of that, it's their fault, all 2 billion of them, when 0.4% of them go out and blow the league up. Fix up, you idiots. Behave yourself because a lot of people have sand for brains and cannot think for themselves so you, yes you, from one part of the world and sect, stop that total stranger from another part of the world and different sect from doing something stupid in another part of the world or you too will be to blame. Oh, and if you fail to stop something that you are powerless to stop, we're coming for that Joint Oil.

Team Criminal/Illegal Immigrants

Next up is the newest/oldest team in the league. I introduce you to, the Illegal Immigrants. Apparently, this team is made

up of rapists and criminals but if you look closely, you might find 1 or 2 good ones. How could I forget? There are terrorists in there as well. This team moves through the league like locusts, raping, terrorizing and…. criminaling (get on it Oxford). They sit at home in their shithole countries, plotting and planning as to which country they want to invade. They go child shopping, looking for the right kid to bring along for sympathy points. They're lazy and unwilling to play by the league rulebook and they are here to …. TAKE…. YOUR……. DJUUUBBBSSSSS… I mean, take your place on the team that you worked so hard for by just being born. Do you know what is worse about team Illegal Immigrants? They bring performance-enhancing drugs into the league by jumping the guard rails without a ticket. They get players hooked on those drugs and hooked on not taking personal responsibility. They dare to bring different perspectives, cultures, and languages to the league as if they own the place. They are simply…. an invading force. Invading force. Hmmm. Sounds familiar.

So, what is the reality when it comes to Team Illegal Immigrants? Was anything stated above true or is it all hyperbole? Well, just like all propaganda, it is an exaggeration with a sprinkling, a dash, a smidgen of truth like salt. Just enough for taste but not enough to overpower that sweet taste of lies and vitriol. Reality is not created equal in the Race League. Some teams are very well equipped, some, not so much and others

dominate the league on a seasonal basis. Some teams are drowning in resources and riches like joint oil but are raided and destabilized by the top teams in the league (now that I think about it, Team Terrorist Muslims and Team Thug Blacks get raided the most). You can't play the game without the proper gear, shoes or even a coach if your top coaches are removed and replaced by bumbling idiots who take bribes from the ruling teams to lose. What is a player to do? Should he/she A. Stay and break every bone in their body and play for a dead-end team that won't bring any championships, B. Revolt, be branded dissidents and removed/blackballed from the league, C. try to find a new team where they can play and rebuild their lives, or D. lash out at those they deem responsible for their ill plight and create a fringe team of extremists to further their cause. Most choose C, believe it or not (No really. They choose C. I said C, not D. It's crazy to think that a human being would try to improve their lives). Let's use a current team as an example of this dynamic.

If you were to ask the league which option Team Terrorist Muslims would take, some would say D. They're leaving their teams to bring terror to other teams because they hate them and everything they stand for. They're looking to bring and impose their playbook on to other teams and force them to play a very defensive and rigid game and **WE CAN'T HAVE THAT IN THIS LEAGUE.**

Or......or.......orrrrrrr........ as mentioned above, their team has been systematically picked apart all for that sweet joint oil. Listen. With joint oil, your joint will feel like the joints of a 20-year-old. It's miraculous stuff and very coveted by the league. Get a bottle today. All it costs is a few lives but they're not yours so, yaaay. Anyway, I digress (this is becoming a common theme isn't it?). Certain teams in the league have decimated Team Muslims for their resources and also because of disdain and hate. The icing on the cake is the demonizing of the team to justify the continuous rape of this team, knowing that some emotional fool will lose his skull and do something stupid. This fool will then be used as an example to further the rape of the team because we can't have these rogue players coming and harming the league. Just like every player in the league though, Team Terrorist Muslims just want to play in peace, using their own playbook just like everybody else. Too bad you guys have that sweet joint oil and other supplements that strengthen other teams in the league and bring in that dolla dolla bill y'all.

Going back to Team Illegal Immigrants as a whole, this team is driven by pure desperation and the most basic human desire, to survive. People travel or move all of the time to better themselves, their family and their lives. In some parts, these people are called expats. In other parts, they're known as vermin or cockroaches. It all depends on how you are

viewed by society and what race you are. This vitriol is driven by leaders of the league spouting hatred and propaganda to get more people to go to their games and buy their shitty merchandise. As mentioned earlier, they use examples of bad behavior by any individual from the other teams as reasons to justify their tactics. **Detour alert. Detour alert.**

THEY...TOOK...OUR...JOOOOBBBSSSSS

I have to get a thought off of my chest. It's been there like mucus that just loves hugs and not letting go. It centers around the notion that immigrants are taking OUR JOOOOOOBSSSS. In this fragile climate, you constantly hear about immigrants going into countries and taking jobs from hard-working natives. They're pushing their way in, kicking down doors and forcing managers and execs to hire them or else they will give their cheap labor to the competition. It's disgusting and must be stopped dammit. These people are not allowed to work and care for themselves as well as their families.

Jobs are not for them. They should stick to being criminals, rapists, and menaces to society. That's their job, to help manufacture the propaganda so that leaders can use it to churn it out and continue the divisions while they run out the back door with all of the money. It's a beautiful system and, more importantly, it works.

Now that I got that out of the way, that was not my initial thought. Here it is. To the people who moan about these outsiders taking the jobs that they probably would never do, have you ever stepped outside of your box to look at the bigger picture? Let's stick with the theme of groups. One group is taking your group's jobs but......would it not be your own group's members that gave those jobs away to the other in the first place? If you are white and you hate the fact that these immigrants are taking your jobs, would it not be a fellow white person who is giving your job away? So, in effect, your fellow man is the problem and not the immigrant.

Do you know why they don't think like you but will talk like you to make you think you were on the same page? Well, they don't think like you because they don't care about you or your desire to work. They only care about their bottom line and who they can exploit because they know certain people are desperate. You see, if they tried any bs with you, you would speak up. There is no way you would accept $4.00 an hour for 20 hours a day of work. The immigrant, on the other hand, would, seeing as he probably lived on water and ice for dinner with a side of steam for dessert.

You see, your fellow man only cares about profits and full pockets. That immigration talk is just for you, the peasant. That racial talk. It's politics (book coming to a

shelf near you). It is to curry your favor while they screw you over because they know how simple and tribal you are. They exploit everyone, immigrant and kinfolk alike.

Why do they side with you in speech only? So that you will never look at them as the problem. If you keep looking at the brown people, they can continue getting that tasty cash. Basically, they create a villain for you to look at while they operate in the shadows. So, the next time Ahmed applies for a job cleaning a KFC bathroom, just remember what I said above. Oh, and I can guarantee that if you had the same thought process as Ahmed and accepted the meager pay and benefits of such a job, you would get it easily too.

Alert. Alert. Course correction. Back on track. The teams mentioned above are not the only teams as different parts of the world have their own Bias League. Just think of any dumbass stereotype of a group that you can and guaranteed a team exists (Not in reality. This section is satire, remember?) So, what am I trying to say after writing all the above? Well, that we're tribal. That's it. The end. Look out for my next volume………. (producer whispers something in my ear). Well, I guess I have more to write about. Sorry about that. Ahem. So, what was I saying? Ah yes. Tribal. We're tribal. The end.

You Are What You Eat. And it Tastes Partisan

If you follow a particular team then you have your source of news. Maybe you like reading the Thug Blacks Gazette or maybe you get your team news from the Racist Whites Sports website. In this league called our world, everyone has a source of information catered to their liking. I mean, if you follow Team Illegal Immigrants why would you care if someone got traded for Team Thug Blacks? You wouldn't even know because you are clearly not going to go and read their newsletter. Moving away from the Team analogy (I can feel the mass triggering) let's look at the world and how people use media, news, and information to confirm and validate their biases.

Now that I am thinking about it, now would have been a good time to use Teams as an analogy to speak about this topic. Dammit, I used all of my chips too soon. I guess I'm going to have to tell it straight. We all have a belief system (Not religious. That is coming in another book) that shapes our view of the world, people in the world and even our place in this world. This belief system is fueled by the media we watch and the information we take in. Do you hate immigrants and want your daily dose of immigrant bashing news? Read the Daily Bail or Sox News (I don't have a lawyer and I am not taking any chances). Everyone has their source and sometimes, these sources mold us more than we realize.

Have you ever spoken to someone or had a debate and said something that was so logical and obvious (to you) that it outraged you when the other person just didn't seem to get it, or they refused to acknowledge it? Man, that is infuriating. How the hell can you NOT SEE THIS? ARGHHHH. It is guaranteed that each person has their own train of thought, bolstered by their own source of information from their own cliques. There is one dynamic in this world that fits this template (And guess what? This will be expanded on in another volume to come. Get your checklist).

I am about to open a can of worms but, that dynamic is the Liberal vs. Conservative dynamic. Left Vs. Right, if you will. Now, before I continue, I just want to say, there is no neutral. There is right and there is wrong. truth and lie. Sorry BNN. (No lawyer. Remember?) Now, why did I have to point out that there is only right and wrong? Because both parties believe wholeheartedly, that they are 100% correct. Both parties' ideas are as similar as bread and the letter V. Wait a minute. If you cut bread diagonally, it can look like a V. Anyway, I digress. These ideologies are very different, but each group firmly believes in their own.

Why am I bringing this up? Well, both groups firmly believe that they are right and the other is wrong. Every piece of information from their sources is correct and everything else

is wrong or fake news (hand gesture). One might see those who are kind, believe in social justice and all that hippy shit as belonging to one ideological group while some might see those who are about individual above all, lovers of no one but their own race/group and dangerously patriotic as belonging to another ideological group. Oh, I won't assign any labels here. I will leave it up to the reader to decide who is who through their own ideological slant and by taking in this information and forming an opinion based on this information, which in turn will be doing exactly what this section is about. You're my Guinea Pigs. MWAH HAHAHAHAHA. Ahem.

Where was I. If a person believes that their ideology is truth, they will also believe that their sources of information are also truth. A person who hates mankind and wants to see people who don't look like them dead are not going to read the teachings of Jesus......wait......some claim to do just that. I think I will have to expand on this in the future in another volume. I will probably call it…. My Observations of Religion. I'm so good at digressing. Back to the subject at hand.

A person with a particular ideology, be it liberal or conservative (Left or right) will most likely only read or watch what confirms their biases. If they tried to do otherwise, they would squirm in their seats, start to sweat profusely and probably start shaking in silent rage like a blender that hasn't

had its coffee for the day. Our ideology has become like a part of our identity and no one likes their identity being threatened. They will fight tooth and nail to defend their identity/ideology. Remember what I said though. There is right and there is wrong.Right and wrong is not determined by a person BELIEVING something is right or wrong. All a person has to do is research to find the truth (what is right). But wait. Is it that simple? A person with an ideology will research, but as said earlier they will research to confirm their bias or twist any new information to fit their bias.

This brings me full circle to the news. No matter what anyone tells you, the news is not unbiased. The news/media will always have a slant towards a political or ideological…. ideology(?) That's not the word I was looking for, but it will do. News agencies will carry water for whatever or whoever they believe in and will present the news to their followers and to fresh minds with this in…. mind. Damn, I did it again. I'm running out of words. Anyway, as I was saying, news agencies depend on the tribalism of the populace to get ratings and to also get their messages across. An example of this can be seen with Box News, BNN and BMNBC (these are real. I promise). Box News hates everyone and everything and pushes a message of fear and division through propaganda and pure lies.

Before I move on, I just have to say, one would think that

spotting blatant lies would be obvious in this day and age with our tidal wave of information. Unfortunately, lies have taken on the appearance of a spy kitted out in a wig and the best disguise seen since a Mission Impossible movie (pick one). Why is it so hard to expose a lie for what it is? Well, a lie is only a lie to a man that knows the truth or believes otherwise from the lie. The truth can become a lie if a man is ignorant or believes otherwise from the truth. It is this way becaaaaauuussseeee...... people have their own ideologies. There is another reason as well. We go with what we want to go with in our hearts and block out anything that challenges that. If you WANT to believe that a certain people are murderous animals who want to take your last cookie and not clean up the crumbs, then you will go to every source that confirms.... that.... bias. It's almost as if this should have a special name. Hmmmm.

Alternately, that very person will ignore any contradicting evidence. Even if one of the people that he hated appeared with a halo, big, feathery wings, and glad tidings, they would find a reason to dismiss what is in front of their eyes. Wings and a halo? They have evolved into mutant chickens and will kill us all! Now, when you have a news cycle and a media that pumps our airwaves full of lies on a consistent basis and questions truth at the same rate then people will be confused. Also, the threat of being labeled

if you believe in the truth (or the lie) is very high. Believe in the truth/lie? You are a social justice warrior, socialist, racist, xenophobe/homophobe. Hearing these smears repeatedly are enough to sway people from the truth or the lie. **Back to our regularly scheduled programming.**

Where was I? As yes. Box news. They push trash. BNN pushes everything because they want everyone to love them. They present the truth and the lie and then say, "Hey. We don't know. It's all even. We are neutral. They try to cast a net to catch all of the fish and in turn, becomes a proponent of false news. Each station has its own clique of followers (Box News has a rabid fanbase, primed and programmed to do the bidding of their dear leader/s). The news is not the only culprit. The internet has been a massive source of information/ misinformation. You just have to go to YouTube to see all of the channels available for anyone with a particular political slant or belief (flat earthers, I'm looking at you). Now here is the thing. Information is readily available, be it on the internet or from the news. All slants and perspectives are out there in the open, for anyone to see and to challenge their own belief system.

Unfortunately, we as humans are not wired that way to challenge our inner core beliefs. Just look at religion as an example (I promise this volume is coming. Stop pressuring me). It would be like treason for a person with a set belief like, let's say, immigration is a bad thing, to go to Sam Seder's or Kyle Kulinski's YouTube channels and listen to their perspective. It would be a travesty to view the statistical evidence that proves your belief system might be flawed.

What do we do in those situations? We gravitate towards statistics that confirm our biases. These statistics are usually doctored or misleading, just to perfectly fit our beliefs like a snug pair of jeans on the ass of ideology. Not only do we as humans gravitate towards skewed stats, but we also cling tightly to anecdotal evidence. What's that? Crime is statically lower in Townsville than in most cities? Well, I call BS because Box News told me that there was a crime spree where 12 Townsvillains (see what I did there? Oh, and it was 1 Townvillain but that doesn't strike terror in the hearts of man) robbed a little old lady of her life savings and pension. Oh, and Greg told me that he heard gunshots near Townsville so it must have been from Townsville so you can take your voodoo statistics from the government and shove them. It makes people so uncomfortable to face any evidence that counters their own belief system.

I DON'T CARE WHAT REALITY SAYS DAMMIT

Now, I'm going to go out on a limb and say that is only the case with people who are wrong and WANT to be wrong. Here's a prime example. I remember watching a news

interview where they were talking about a certain event involving immigration. The interviewee poignantly explained how she had no problem with these immigrants coming into her country the legal way and by following the law instead of crossing the border illegally. The interviewer calmly told her that the people who were the subject of the discussion had done just that. They tried to enter legally through a port of entry. The interviewee's tone and the message changed drastically with this new information. She proceeded to say she didn't want them in the country. Deep down in her heart, this is what she wanted. For the scary people to stay on their side of the line but, you see, people find it hard to be true to themselves because they do not want to be called out (we as humans do not like being called something taboo or bad).

They try to hide their true nature behind a faux display of virtue. This is why so many racists and heartless people hide behind the fake persona of being religious, patriotic or any "positive" moniker that you can think of. It helps them to feel righteous in their badness and it also helps the people around them to feel comfortable with the surface level display of virtue that hides the underbelly of corruption and moral bankruptcy. Ever wondered why such people are some of the most judgmental people on this planet? They have bought into their self-righteousness and see others that do what's bad in their eyes (a lot of the time they are doing the exact same bs) as being lesser than them and worthy of scorn. They would never apply that standard to themselves because, well, they are righteous, of course. The interviewee mentioned above started off virtuous and "reasonable", but the truth quickly brought out the inner bigotry in her. Can such people be saved?

No amount of truth, evidence or information will change such a person. The only thing that will change a person with that mindset is their conscious decision to change and to stop lying to themselves (something we tend to do on a daily).

With this in mind, can people be reached? Again, it depends on the heart of the person. Some people are just misguided but open to correction and guidance. The problem that arises is associations. It is hard for people to stray from the thought process of the pack in fear of ostracism. Some people cling to false beliefs because they want to belong. Some discard their ideology and their friends that shared the same ideology and find new friends. For the most part though, people stick to what they want to. For example, do you think some Nazis do not know that their ideology is trash? Of course they do but it allows them to hate and that is what is more important to them.

As of writing, there are certain world leaders who have zero discernable qualities but have a cult-like following because they legitimize the bias and hatred within them so, no matter

how many lies they tell, no matter how many crimes or scandals they are caught up in, the followers turn a blind eye and even defend the person because they allow them to be the worst versions of themselves (this should all be in the politics volume…coming soon). This is how it is with cults of personality. Our make up as human beings make it hard to break the formatting of our brains. Because of this, there will always be factions, divisions, hatred, and groupthink. That doesn't mean people can't or shouldn't change. History has taught us that one man can change and define a whole generation (Vanilla Ice, I'm looking at you).

Well, that was a mouthful. A lot was covered in this volume from how we are influenced by the society around us, how we view each other to how we take in information that confirms our biases. Is there any hope for us as humans? No matter what I write here, people will believe what they want to believe, hate who they want to hate and follow who they want to follow. Ignorance has become a luxury in this word and sometimes it's hard to tell people to give up their comfort and luxury. I could tell people to be more cognizant of reality and the different examples in society that challenge their narrow beliefs about people etc. I could say remove yourselves from the restrictive bubble of the media and groupthink. I could even say to judge people as individuals and not as a straw man collective to be torn down. I could say all of these things but, this is merely one book among a sea of contrary bs. There is also the battle against basic human nature and the inner stubbornness against change and the "other" narrative that we all either struggle with or embrace wholeheartedly.

I know people with a certain mindset will dismiss the contents of this book (they might not even get past the first 3 pages) or embrace it. That won't change. We are people. We are mentally flawed, brainwashed, misguided, enlightened, chose an appropriate word and place it here. All we can do is in the least, make people think if they want to. I could post this to social media and algorithms will make sure that it reaches people who agree with the message inside while cutting out the people that probably need this perspective in life. We are all funneled towards what we already like and agree with and not towards stuff that would make us feel uncomfortable and think. It doesn't mean you don't write, record or get your message out though. Like I said above, one person can define a generation so all of the fighters of human BS, keep doing what you are doing. You may not be able to change the world but you can change a person, who in turn can change those around them. Create the domino effect. Now go out there **AND BE SOMEBODY.**

Director walks over and whispers in my ear. Oh, there's more? Well, this is awkward....again. According to my producers I am contractually obligated to talk about one more subject matter. I guess I'll have to cancel my flight to Fiji. Sigh. Well, where was I? The next topic I will cover is....

Your Pain is My Pleasure, but MY PAIN IS...

An injustice. I am about to open another can of worms here. Buckle up, Dorothy. We're about to go to Kansas.

The world has changed a lot over the last few decades. People have traveled and set up home in different countries. Children have been born and have become citizens in countries other than the ones of their parent's birth. For example, England, the country of my birth is home to many races and cultures from Indian and African to Caribbean and Polish. Many countries in the world share this dynamic from the USA to the Caribbean and even Europe. As they say, the world has become a melting pot of people. With a melting pot comes clashes and sometimes division. Some cultures butt heads or the natives of a country resent the notion that other people and cultures are in their country.

Some races and cultures put up with terrible racism and bigotry that no human being should not have to put up with. Now, I bet you think you know where I am going with this. Mmm mmm. You don't. Here comes the swerve.

People are very reactive to the bigotry they and their community receive. They become vocal about it and even march against it. For instance, Indians, Pakistanis, etc. might speak out against the bigotry that they face, and they should. They should speak up and bring attention to it. Too bad that rarely translates over to the people THEY hate. What do I mean about that? Well, everybody seems to hate everybody. The Asians complaining about racism would hate people from the Black community or anyone darker. In parts of their country, a caste system is in place where the darker you are, the lower you are on the social ladder. For a lot of the human race, the awareness to the bigotry they face is totally selfish and doesn't leave their circle. This is just one example of that dynamic. Persecuted West Indians would be bigoted to Africans or Black people would be bigoted to whoever is the immigrant of the month. Of course, this is not the case for everyone. Some people are kind to others because of the bigotry they face. Their empathy chip works.

Others, on the other hand, are completely oblivious to the irony of hating on other races and cultures while they simultaneously complain about the bigotry that they face.

This happens in religion too (which blows my mind). Some Asian Muslims will lose their minds to the fact that their daughter or son is in love with a Black Muslim. This happens in Christianity as well. Some Christians go and hear the word of God speak about humanity loving each other but will still object to someone in their family being in a relationship with someone of a different race. Of course, these same people will be cognizant of the bigotry they face as a Muslim, Christian, Black or Asian person, but are completely unaware of their own bigotry. How I see it if you are hating on a people, culture or a religion but are unhappy at the racism or bigotry you face then you need to clean your own house or accept the karma that you are experiencing. You cannot have your hate cake and eat it too. Before you fight against the people that hurt you, look to see who you are hurting first. Oh and, to those who follow a caste system and treat your fellow human beings like animals because they have more melanin than you, donate your brains to science. You don't need them and you're not using them. Also, you're scum if you treat someone like a subhuman because of something as arbitrary and asinine as skin color. Never forget that the same was done to you and millions of your people were murdered for the exact same reasons. Be smarter. Be wiser and also, gain a heart because at this moment, you do not have one and you forfeit your own humanity by your hateful actions. This goes for anyone who treats another poorly because of their culture and/or skin color. Fix up or don't complain about what you go through. Have some empathy. Absorb what you go through and project that ill feeling towards the ones you also mistreat. Realize that you are what you hate and change it within. If you find that you can't ever like these black people, or these Africans or the Polish, shut up and accept the hate that comes your way. Avoid hypocrisy and accept that bigotry like a man/woman.

Ok. I think I'm done now. Checks with publishers. Yep. I'm done. I hope you learned something from this book or that it gave you a different perspective on life. That was the goal and I hope it was achieved. I now must go into my basement, light my candle, get my ink and feather and start writing the next volume. Hope to see you again.